SUPER CUTE!

Baby Lions

by Christina Leaf

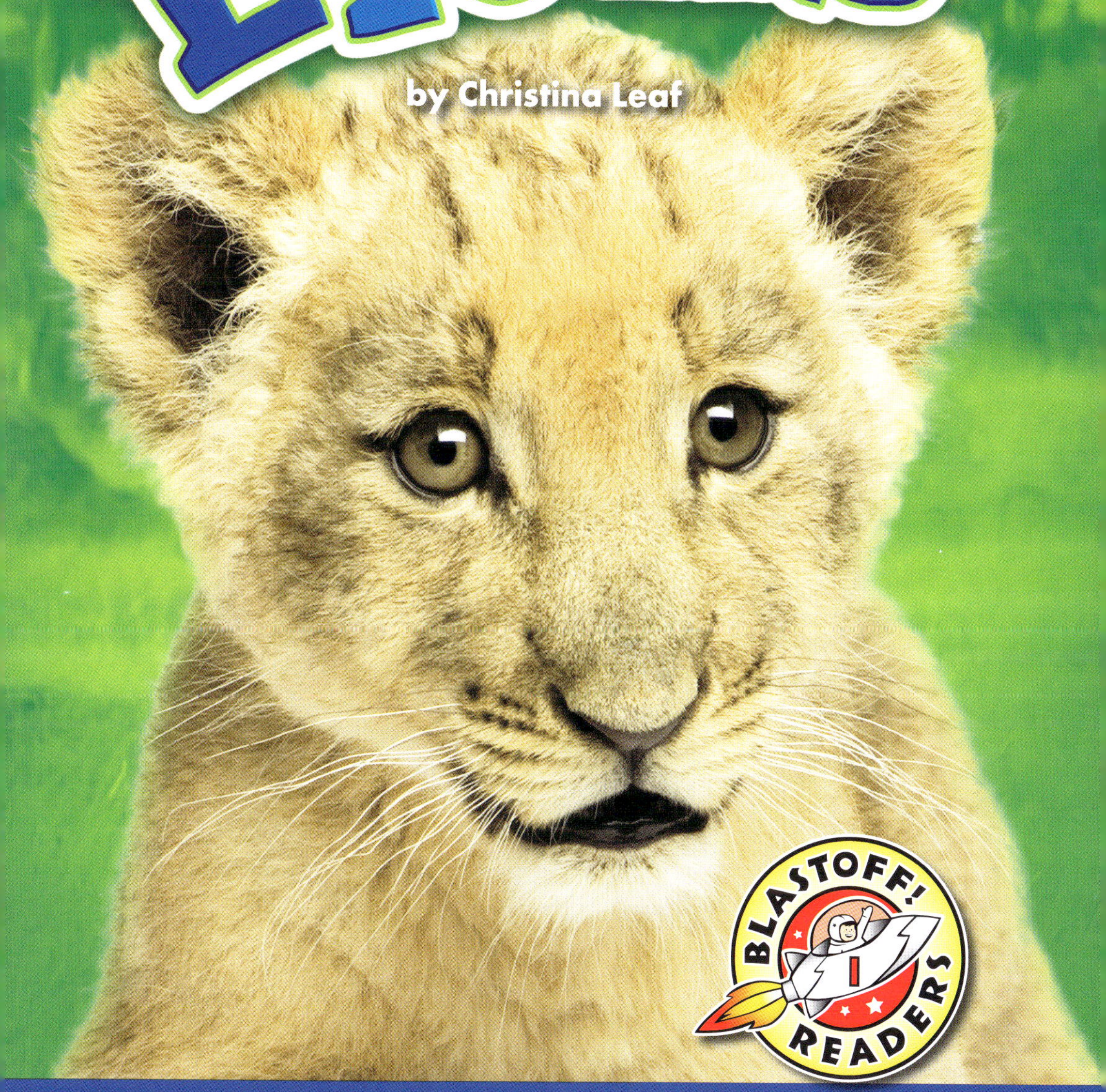

BELLWETHER MEDIA • MINNEAPOLIS, MN

Note to Librarians, Teachers, and Parents:

Blastoff! Readers are carefully developed by literacy experts and combine standards-based content with developmentally appropriate text.

Level 1 provides the most support through repetition of high-frequency words, light text, predictable sentence patterns, and strong visual support.

Level 2 offers early readers a bit more challenge through varied simple sentences, increased text load, and less repetition of high-frequency words.

Level 3 advances early-fluent readers toward fluency through increased text and concept load, less reliance on visuals, longer sentences, and more literary language.

Level 4 builds reading stamina by providing more text per page, increased use of punctuation, greater variation in sentence patterns, and increasingly challenging vocabulary.

Level 5 encourages children to move from "learning to read" to "reading to learn" by providing even more text, varied writing styles, and less familiar topics.

Whichever book is right for your reader, Blastoff! Readers are the perfect books to build confidence and encourage a love of reading that will last a lifetime!

This edition first published in 2014 by Bellwether Media, Inc.

Library of Congress Cataloging-in-Publication Data

Leaf, Christina, author.
Baby Lions / by Christina Leaf.
pages cm. – (Blastoff! Readers. Super Cute!)
Summary: "Developed by literacy experts for students in kindergarten through grade three, this book introduces baby lions to young readers through leveled text and related photos"– Provided by publisher.
Audience: Ages 5-8.
Audience: K to grade 3.
Includes bibliographical references and index.
ISBN 978-1-60014-974-0 (hardcover : alk. paper)
1. Lion–Infancy–Juvenile literature. [1. Animals–Infancy.] I. Title.
QL737.C23L42 2014
599.757'139–dc23
2013050255

Printed in the United States of America, North Mankato, MN.

Table of Contents

Cubs!

Baby lions are called cubs. They are born in **litters** of two to four babies.

Life in the Pride

Lion cubs live in **prides**. A pride can have many litters and mothers.

Each mom cares for her own litter. The moms work together to **protect** their cubs from danger.

Newborn cubs drink their mom's milk. Older cubs eat with the big lions.

Mom keeps her cubs clean. She licks their fur.

Cubs need a lot of rest. They snuggle close to one another.

Playtime

Lion cubs love to run and jump. Brothers and sisters **wrestle**.

Playful cubs also copy mom and dad. They **pretend** to hunt.

This cub wants
to be like dad.
He shows his
scariest face.
ROAR!

Glossary

litters—groups of babies that are born together

newborn—just born

pretend—to make believe

prides—groups of lions

protect—to keep safe

wrestle—to fight in a playful way

To Learn More

AT THE LIBRARY

Clark, Willow. *Lions: Life in the Pride.* New York, N.Y.: PowerKids Press, 2011.

Owen, Ruth. *Lion Cubs.* New York, N.Y.: Bearport Pub., 2011.

Zobel, Derek. *Lions.* Minneapolis, Minn.: Bellwether Media, 2012.

ON THE WEB

Learning more about lions is as easy as 1, 2, 3.

1. Go to www.factsurfer.com.
2. Enter "lions" into the search box.
3. Click the "Surf" button and you will see a list of related web sites.

With factsurfer.com, finding more information is just a click away.

Index

The images in this book are reproduced through the courtesy of: Eric Isselee, front cover; dean bertoncelj, pp. 4-5; Biosphoto/ SuperStock, pp. 6-7, 8-9; Minden Pictures/ SuperStock, pp. 10-11; Steve Bloom Images/ SuperStock, pp. 12-13; skynesher, pp. 14-15; Gerard Lacz/ Kimballstock, pp. 16-17; Art Wolfe Stock/ Cultura Limited/ SuperStock, pp. 18-19; Malcolm Schuyl/ FLPA, pp. 20-21.